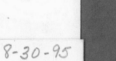

EYES

Published by Doubleday, a division of
Bantam Doubleday Dell Publishing Group, Inc.,
666 Fifth Avenue, New York, New York 10103

Doubleday and the portrayal of an anchor with a dolphin
are trademarks of Doubleday, a division
of Bantam Doubleday Dell Publishing Group, Inc.

Library of Congress Cataloging-in-Publication Data
Worthy, Judith.
Eyes/by Judith Worthy; illustrated by Béba Hall.
p.   cm.
Summary: Illustrations and text in verse describe the eyes of
various animals, including insects, and how the eyes are keys to
certain characteristics of the animals.
1. Eye—Juvenile literature.   2. Animals—Juvenile literature.
[1. Eye. 2. Animals.]   I. Hall, Béba, ill.   II. Title.
QP475.7.W67   1989
591.19'153—dc19
88-18809
CIP
AC
ISBN 0-385-24965-9
ISBN 0-385-24966-7 (lib. bdg.)

Text copyright © 1988 Judith Worthy
Illustrations copyright © 1988 Béba Hall

First published in 1988 by Ashton Scholastic Pty. Limited (Inc. in
New South Wales), P.O. Box 579, Gosford 2250. Also in Brisbane, Melbourne,
Adelaide, Perth, and Auckland, New Zealand

EYES

by Judith Worthy
illustrated by Béba Hall

DOUBLEDAY

NEW YORK LONDON TORONTO SYDNEY AUCKLAND

An owl has eyes
     that glow at night,
          To give the frogs
               and mice a fright.

This frog
    has enormous bulging eyes.
    Surely too big
        for a creature its size!

The elephant
    is huge and wise,
        With lots of secrets
            in its eyes.

You have to be quick
to catch the eye of a mouse,
One whisker-flick
and it's back in its house.

Cats' eyes can be green
or gold or blue,
And they glow at night
when they look at you.

This dog has eyes
that seem to say,
'Come on! Hurry up!
I want to play!'

See the hungry glint
in a spider's eyes.
But he won't eat you!
He's looking for flies.

A fly's eye is many eyes
        it's true,
            And each tiny eye
                sees a part of the view.

Some fish
        though only small in size,
                Have the most
                        enormous eyes.

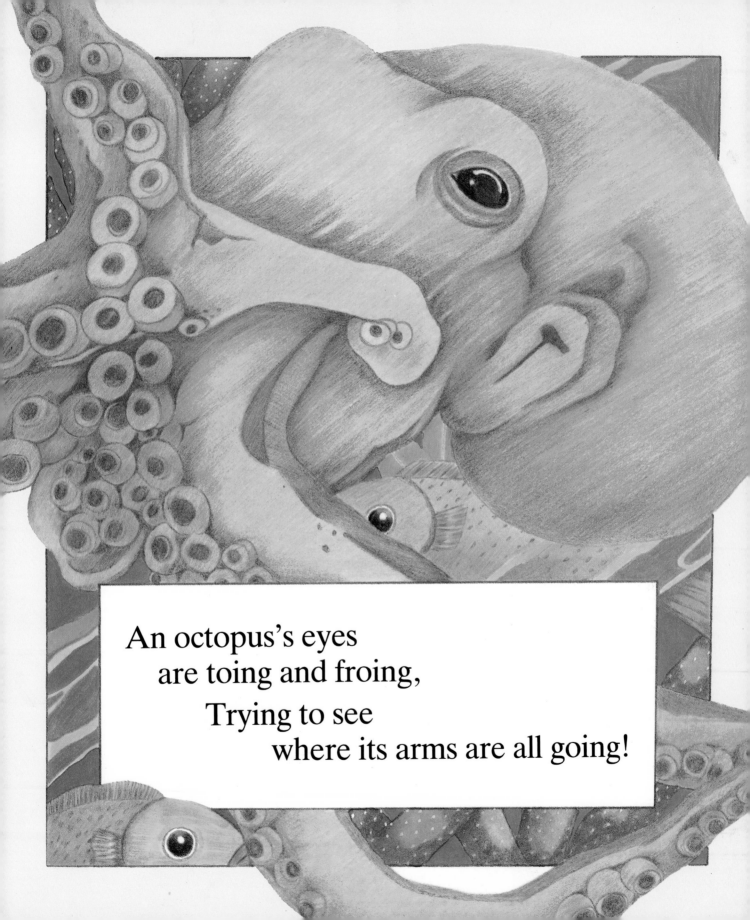

An octopus's eyes
  are toing and froing,
    Trying to see
      where its arms are all going!

Take a look
    at a camel's eyes.
        Are those long lashes
            to keep off the flies?

There's a wary look
    in an emu's eye,
        Perhaps because
            this bird can't fly.

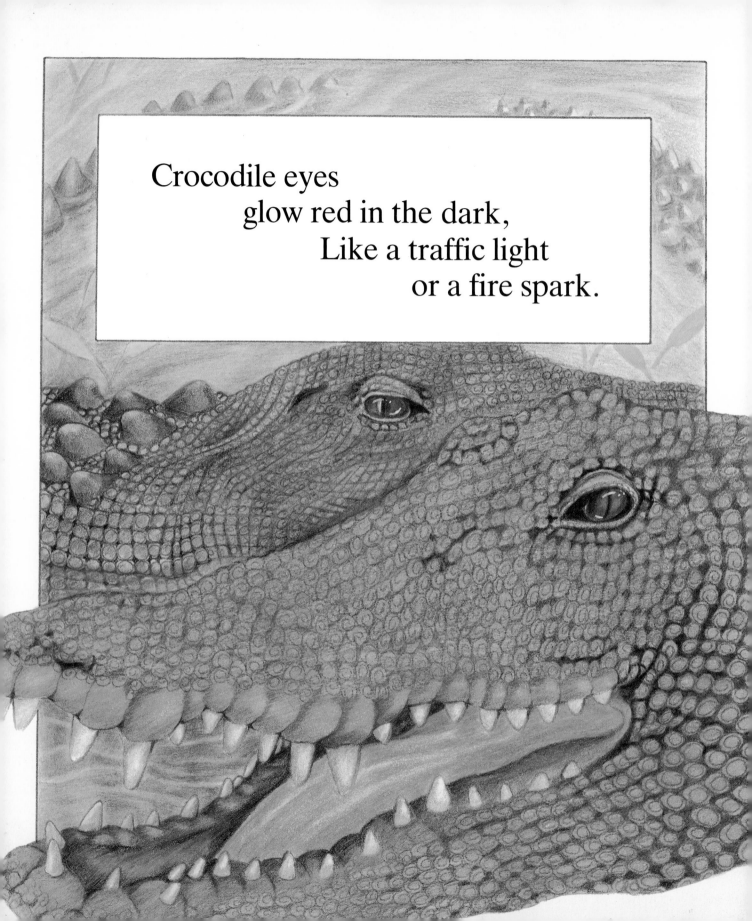

Crocodile eyes
 glow red in the dark,
  Like a traffic light
   or a fire spark.

Though this tortoise looks
for somewhere to hide,
Its shell is right there
and it's safe inside!

The eyes of a tiger
 are yellow with rage,
  When it cannot roam free
   but is kept in a cage.

Giraffes have large eyes
so soft and brown,
And you see them best
when giraffes look down.

You have to crouch down
very low to see,
The busy eyes
of the honey-bee.

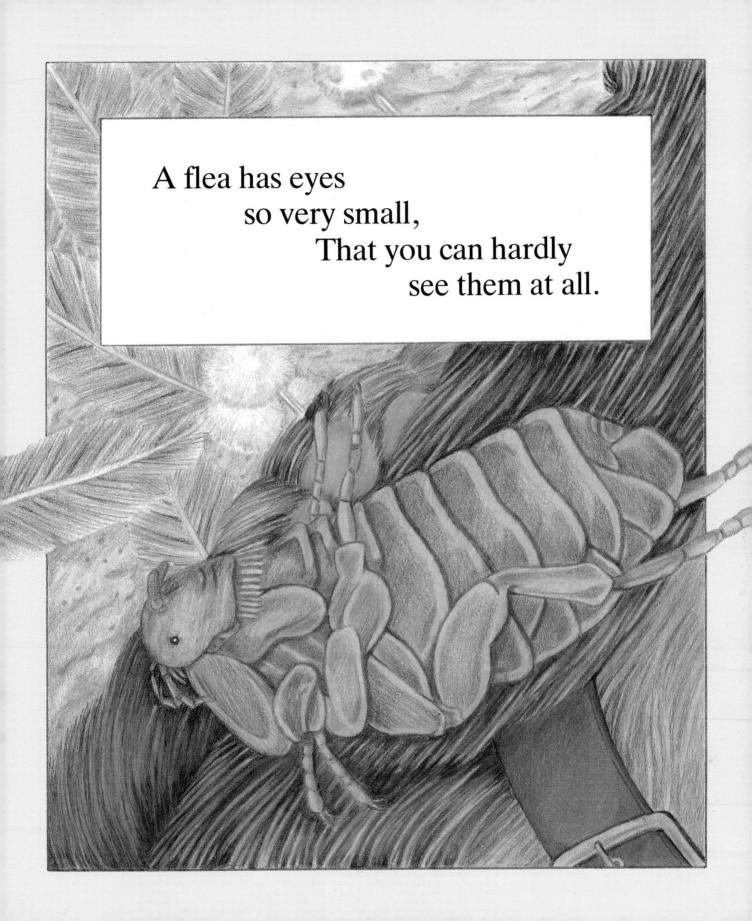

A flea has eyes
    so very small,
        That you can hardly
            see them at all.

Butterfly fish
    have false eyes on their tails,
        To frighten off sharks
            and stingrays and whales.

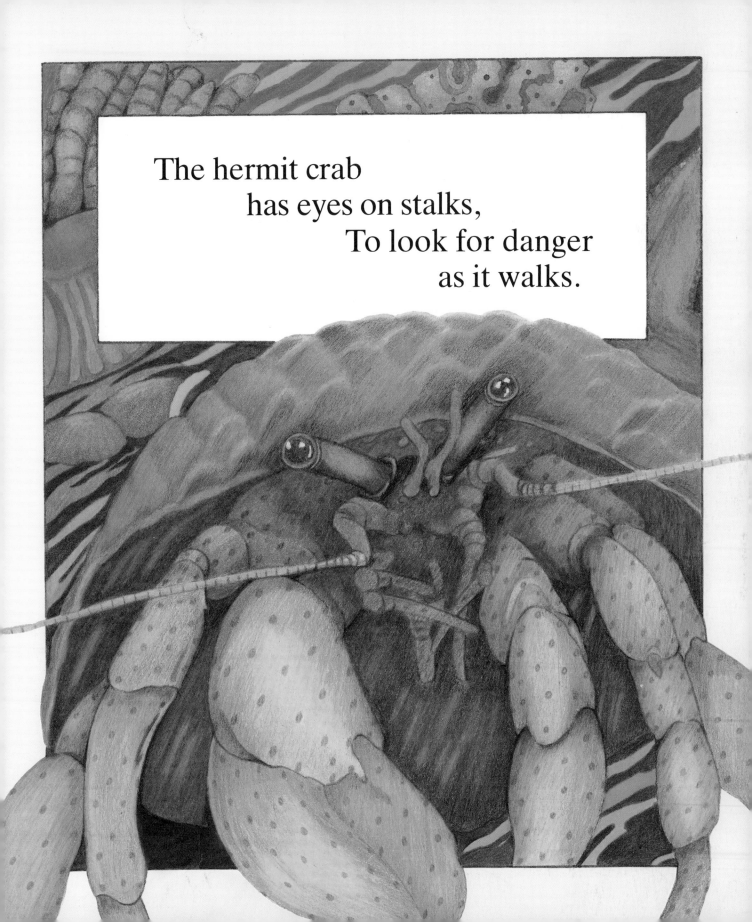

The hermit crab
has eyes on stalks,
To look for danger
as it walks.

Never mind
    how hard it tries,
        The carpet snake
            can't blink its eyes.

A possum's eyes
    are huge and bright,
        So it can see
            on the darkest night.

The eyes of a dolphin
seem to smile.
It wants you to jump in
and play for a while.

The eyes of the flying fox
help it to see
The fruit it eats
as it hangs from the tree.

The emperor moth
has large painted eyes.
Don't be fooled —
that's a clever disguise!

An eagle
soaring in the blue,
Has the highest
bird's-eye view.

A lizard blinks
    a sleepy eye,
        But soon wakes up
            to snatch a fly.

Now go to a mirror,
   What do you see?
      Your own eyes of course,
         Which are 'Just right for me!'

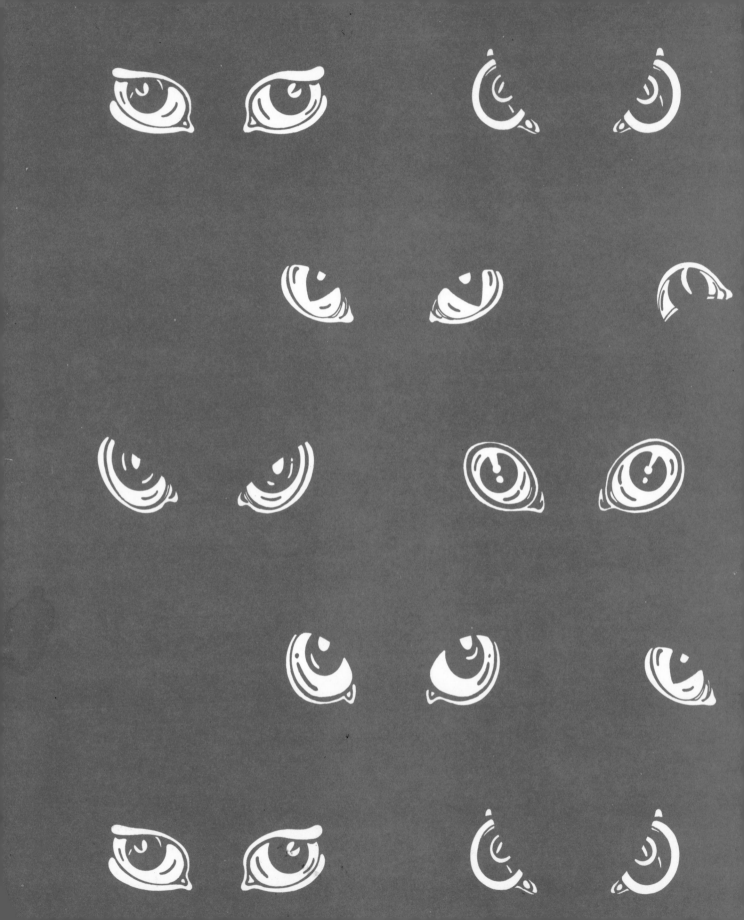